MEN, LET'S TALK!

PORNOGRAPHY:
THE QUIET ADDICTION

By

D0792587

Fitzhugh G. Houston

An inspirational testimony about the 20-year struggle with addiction to pornography, and how being born again led to eventual deliverance through his relationship with Jesus Christ and the power of the Word of God.

C 2003

SECOND EDITION

HSU

HOUSTON SPECTRUM PUBLICATIONS

Men, Let's Talk
PORNOGRAPHY:
The Quiet Addiction

©Copyright 2003 by Fitzhugh G. Houston
Published by Houston Spectrum Publications
Panorama City, California 91402
www.menletstalk.org
Library of Congress Cataloging-in-Publication Data
Houston, Fitzhugh G.
Men, Let's Talk / Fitzhugh G. Houston

People Are Talking
about MEN, LET'S TALK!

"A gripping display of honesty, transparency and enlightenment.."

"comes straight from the heart"

"...right on target. This is needed."

"God is sure to set free, bless and help others through this book."

"I was delivered from the spirit of lust within a week after reading it"

"A courageous first effort by the author."

Table Of Contents

Preface

Foreward

Chapter 1   The Shocker: How It All Began   13

Chapter 2   Moving On Up To The Big Time!   17

Chapter 3   A World Full Of Corruption   21

Chapter 4   A New Direction   27

Chapter 5   Uncharted Territory   35

Chapter 6   So Where Do We Go From Here?   41

Chapter 7   The Victory Can Be Yours Right Now   43

Chapter 8   Scriptures For The Battle With Lust   47

Chapter 9   Statistics: The Pornography Industry   51

Chapter 10   Self-Evaluation & Observation   53

About The Author

PREFACE

This book was planted in my spirit in 1996, written four years later but not published until three years after that. What took so long to write it? To be quite honest, I fought it, refused to write it until the Lord firmly persuaded me to do otherwise. The topic is a very sensitive issue for men. I know because I was addicted to pornography for almost 30 years. Most of those years, I was in denial that such an addiction actually exists. I was not able to get a grip on this addiction until I realized it was, in fact, an addiction and, that its effect goes far beyond simply how it consumes you. It also affects your view on life and those around you. Especially your intimate relationships, like marriage.

In order to write this book, I had to get "me" out of the way. I felt ashamed and embarrassed that this addiction had me for so long, well into my years after being saved.

Then the Lord revealed to me that me being delivered from this addiction is much bigger than I am. I needed to reveal my past addiction and my deliverance so that countless other men trapped in this silent addiction can see that they are not alone. Men, there is a way out through Christ Jesus.

Daily, over a period of several weeks the Lord urged me to get started on this book. It was as if the computer had been talking to me every time I passed it saying, "Oh Fitz, God is waiting for your book." But for four years, my pride refused to let me go forth and be obedient to the Lord's voice.

Fours years later, the Lord convicted me during Sunday school class. The Holy Spirit practically pushed me up to the front of the class during testimony time. It was there that I openly revealed that I was a 30 year pornography addict who successfully overcame the addiction through the Word of God. I broke down into tears as the Holy Spirit continued to speak through me about this problem that is running rampant among men, both the saved and the unsaved.

At the conclusion of the class, several women thanked me for bringing the problem to the forefront and admitting that it even exists. One woman told me my testimony gave her a renewed faith in men. Still another woman had just ministered to one of her girlfriends the previous night who was at a loss as to how to deal with her husband who was addicted to pornography.

I finished my testimony by promising in front of the class that I was going to be obedient from this point on and finish the book.

As I finished my tearful testimony, I opened my eyes to find about fifteen male classmates standing behind me supporting me in bringing this problem to the forefront. All of the men grew closer spiritually that day.

I then realized the severity of getting this book written. Since that time, the Lord has brought into my life a number of miracles and incredible blessings. I am convinced these blessings have been the direct result of obeying Him and furthering His work through the writing of this book.

Fearing that disobedience would block any more of God's incredible blessings that have been coming my way, and any possible Jonah experience that could result in my ignoring God's assignment to write this book, here it is.

This book is of course, written from my own life-changing personal experiences and revelations as well as experiences of friends who were also addicted at the time. I hold no punches in the process of sharing this with you. I want you to truly understand the devastating stronghold this addiction has on its victims.

This book may not be for everyone. Some may begin reading out of curiosity, then lay it down as denial takes over and miss their deliverance. But *trust me*, EVERYBODY who reads this book knows somebody who needs it.

Though this book is entitled **MEN, LET'S TALK**, the same addiction effects women as well, either being addicted themselves or being effected indirectly by the addiction through a spouse or loved one. May you find this book informative and helpful and may it truly be a blessing for you, a loved one or someone you know who needs it.

---- *Fitz Houston* ----

FOREWARD

I will never forget that Sunday....the day my husband revealed to our Overcomers' Sunday school class that he had been delivered from an addiction. Just the word "addiction" made the room fall silent. I heard several people draw in a breath, because everyone assumes that addiction means to some kind of drug. And of all people, for the beloved worship service horn player and gospel aerobics teacher to have a drug problem? Oh, no! But there he stood in obedience to God, tears streaming down his face, surrounded in a supportive circle of all his male classmates, as he haltingly blurted out his history of addiction to pornography! I was stunned. I had no idea this was coming. Moments earlier he had been squirming in his seat, mumbling to me that the Lord was telling him to go forward and say something he really didn't want to. I urged him to obey the Lord, until he finally walked forward and was the last person to give a testimony. It was as if the Lord had kept testimonies going, waiting for my husband to come forward, before our teacher moved on to our lesson.

"I didn't want people to know this about me," Fitz told the class, as I smiled at him through tears of my own and resisted my urge to run to his side. "Because of that, I have put off writing a book about it that the Lord has been telling me to write for four years."

So many lives were touched that morning, and a huge breakthrough took place in my husband's walk with the Lord. Talking about being used in a mighty way! I was never more proud of him than I was on that day...and never more humbled as a wife. Many female classmates encouraged him, begged him to finish the book. Women really want to understand. Many of the men thanked him for having the courage to bring this "silent addiction" out into the open in the body of Christ. What safer place should there be to do it?

For every man who has ever wrestled with addiction to porn, thinks he doesn't have a problem, or wants to break free, this book is honest and no holds barred. For all of you ladies, whether you are married or in a relationship with a man who "buys PLAYBOY for the articles," keeps a stash of videos, wants you to perform what you consider "strange things" in bed, please read this book. This is a book to be read AND shared. Someone you know or know of is looking for answers or needs deliverance.

- Jahna Houston -

CHAPTER ONE
The Shocker: How it all Began

Let me explain right now that you'll be seeing the words intercourse, erection, masturbation or self-gratification and throughout this book. Being shy about discussing the addiction to pornography is one thing but being ignorant about it can be a devastating mistake.

One thing needs to be explained up front. "Addicted to pornography" is not the real description of what's going on with men. The porn leads to a type of sexual arousal that must be fulfilled through masturbation or sexual intercourse. The ecstasy experienced from that sequence of events is truly what the addiction is. Masturbation is such a "taboo", "hush-hush" topic that I thought it best not to put it on the cover. The Word has a lot to say about a variety of sexual behaviors which many people wish to justify to themselves saying "it is not covered in the Bible," so that they may continue their immoral behavior.

"But I say to you that whoever looks at a

woman to lust for her has already committed

adultery with her in his heart."

(Matt. 6:28)

"Beloved, I beg you as sojourners and pilgrims,abstain from fleshly lusts which war against the soul."

(1 Peter 2:9)

"For this is the will of God, your sanctification that you should abstain from sexual immorality; that each of you should know how to possess his own vessel in sanctification and honor, not in passion of lust, like the Gentiles who do not know God."

(1 Thess. 4:5)

Coming into my teenage years, I was, like other teenage <u>boys,</u> trying to understand this new incredible surge of hormonal activity taking place in my body, in particular, sexual energy. Girls suddenly went from being annoying pests to attractive beings. Suddenly, now just the thought of a girl in a short dress would get my hormones racing and give me an instant erection, sometimes in the most inconvenient locations.

It was quite frustrating at first for it seemed that my penis had a mind of its own. An erection would pop up for all sorts of reasons. Sometimes it would be triggered by a girl in a short dress, the thought of a girl in a short dress, pictures of a girls in a short dress or swimsuit or tight pants that rubbed me the wrong way as I walked, sitting innocently in class, washing myself in the shower, or simply that morning erection that is with you many times during your waking hours.

Regardless of the reason, this arousal seemed to happen at any time of day, home or at school. It was quite embarrassing. My only defense was to have a book handy to hide behind or constantly have my hands in my pockets trying to hide the bulge.

At age 13 I remember reading what seemed like at the time, a harmless issue of Ebony magazine. I then turned the page and discovered that this issue was the swimsuit issue. Pages and pages of women were dressed in a variety of provocative one-piece swimsuits. They were nothing like swimsuits today.

My hormones went crazy. Here were a variety of pictures of well-developed women posing in positions I'd never paid attention to before but were now quite arousing. Sure enough, the good old dependable erection quickly followed.

Next thing I knew I was helping the arousal along by rubbing my erection against the pillow next to me as I continued to look at the various pictures. Before I knew it, I had ejaculated and a new discovery of pleasure was born.

This newfound pleasure was quite a discovery, almost like a high without dealing with drugs or alcohol. However, there was a similarity. After several dates with the swimsuit issue, I became board and sought to find new pictures for stimulation. Next I found myself looking for anything else with pictures like that swimsuit issue. One day after an exhaustive search, I stumbled up on a Spiegel catalog. It was indeed boring until I found the bra section with several pages of women, twenty to thirty pictures on a page. There were all types of bras, various sizes of breasts and various amounts of exposure. For me and my newfound erotic activity, the bra section was like finding a gold mine. It would be months before I would get bored with all those pictures. Little did I know that this was the first step towards becoming addicted to pornography.

I define masturbation as "deliberate self-stimulation which is designed to achieve sexual arousal or self-gratification." This, of course, does not include wet dreams or surprising ejaculations which occur simply because of your newly discovered sensations and hormone drive during the teenage years. In fact, the do's or don'ts of the act of masturbation is such a controversial topic that I'm only going to deal with it in this book in regards to it's relationship with being addicted to pornography.

During the early teenage years, I was rather shy towards girls and the whole sex issue. So, as a result, the lingerie section of the Spiegel catalog became my fantasy gigolo relationship with women. I never had to worry about rejection or what to say to them with the goal of having sex. The pictures of women wearing bras on the page were all I needed to arouse me enough to ejaculate and I was satisfied with that.

That was back in 1965. My addiction to pornography started innocently enough, from a swimsuit issue of one piece bathing suits, which was all I knew about then. The chances for teens as well as adults to become addicted to pornography today is twice as likely because swimsuits are now much more revealing, while hard and soft pornography is more graphic.

Adult films are now as accessible as renting your favorite movie from the video rental store. And even music videos use sex to increase their sales amongst their main targets, our teenagers. Now, in the 21st century, we are all bombarded by seductive music videos, TV censorship that allows skimpy bikini's and partially nude bodies to run freely on regular television; motion pictures and television shows which leave little to the imagination in their sex scenes, talk shows revealing all sorts of sexual perversions, pornography over the Internet, pornography videos and magazines on sale at your local newsstand. And what has made it even worse today is the growth of the most perverse pornography of all, child pornography. Images of nude children fed to the United States over the Internet from countries overseas who feel that child porn is perfectly acceptable.

And with all this comes the frightening viewpoint from many parents that "kids are going to see this sooner or later anyway. So why not now."

You can probably count on one hand with several fingers left over, the number of films or TV shows that don't suggest a sexual encounter of some sort in their story line.

Film and TV before the 70's barely showed two people kissing with couples sleeping in separate beds. Sex was just insinuated sex, leaving much to the imagination.

Today the theme seems to be, "let's show you as much as we can" before the censors complain.

What happened next? Read on!

CHAPTER TWO

Promotion Time:
Moving on up to the big time

Graduation from high school finally arrived. Hoorah! I'm grown now! Shoot, you can't tell me anything now! I'm ready for the world! Ha!

Being out of high school gives us a false sense of security that we're adults. Even the law doesn't recognize that until the age of twenty-one. Nonetheless, it's a chance to go out on your own so to speak, whether off to college or attempting to move out from your parents into your own place with a roommate.

For me, I was off to college. As far as I was concerned, I was on my own. Independence, wow, what a concept! What did all this have to do with my addiction?

Well first of all, it meant that I could now buy books from the pornography stand. I was raised by my mother most of my life. There was definitely no Playboy magazine lying around the house as some of my other friends had told me about.

By this time, I had graduated to the point where swimsuit issues, bras sections and lingerie, of every type, was a bore. I needed to see women completely naked now in order to get aroused. Pornography addiction like sex addiction is as bad as drugs. The more you get, the more you want.

In the pornography section, I was like a kid in a candy store. There was all black pornography, interracial pornography, white pornography and every kind of sexual perversion imaginable. Thank God, I didn't care for the perverted or freaky stuff. My next order of progression was Playboy, Hustler, Adam and Players (an all black Playboy) magazines. My addiction was quickly getting out of control. I collected centerfolds like a stamp collector collects stamps with the justification that I considered the naked female body to be a work of art. Right! What a load of bull.

The addiction continued. I moved up from porn magazines to porn pictorials, with nothing but pictures of fine naked women posing in seductive positions satisfying my addiction. Why try to fool myself or anyone else? I could care less about the articles. Give me the flesh. I couldn't get enough. I decided to make the porn centerfolds my wallpaper on the walls and ceiling of my room in college.

When girls came to visit my room, it never dawned on me that they would feel uncomfortable, but that they would get the hint and assume the position because I was only interested in what they had under their clothes.

Thinking back, almost every man I knew at that time, did the same thing in their own way. However, I was still rather timid with talking to women. My past six years had been dominated by my real reason for the addiction to pornography: "pictures-arousal-masturbation addiction." I had no idea what else a couple had to talk about if it didn't lead to sex.

As I mentioned in chapter one, this addiction has two sub-descriptions. One sub-description is "pictures-arousal-masturbation" addiction the other is "pictures-arousal-sex" addiction. In either case, sexual fulfillment is the goal. I do not use the phrase "making love" because that description is reserved for two people who are in love. "Sex", as referred to by many people, is simply the act of sexual fulfillment or intercourse without the necessity of any emotional attachment.

Throughout college, a pattern was developing that I was never aware of until after being delivered from this addiction and ministering to others recently.

The type of women I dated closely resembled the women in the magazines and I expected them to behave however my addiction fantasies dictated. I don't have to tell you how many relationships were broken because of the ridiculous pressure I was placing on those women. They could never live up to the expectations of my fantasy life and I didn't even give them a chance to. This is the same kind of pressure placed on wives if their husbands are addicted to pornography.

I eventually learned that in order to have any kind of worthwhile relationship with a real woman, the pictorial wallpaper was going to have to go. This bombardment of flesh twenty-four hours a day had caused a new problem. I looked at every woman as a sex object and not a person with feelings and depth.

Even after successfully replacing the wallpaper with more meaningful athletic and positive images, I kept volumes of magazines in my desk drawer, never more than an arms length away. Feeling now that I was ready for anything. I felt I was now grown enough to go to one of the local Triple "X"- rated hard core pornography theaters. I feel it is important at this point in the book that I explain the difference between "soft core" and "hardcore " pornography.

"Soft-core" porn is partial nudity in seductive poses, nudity and/or couples in provocative sexual positions without showing any genitals in the act of intercourse.

"Hard-core" porn is graphic nude pictorials and positions including the genitals in the act of intercourse or masturbation and every other detail that can or cannot be imagined. Very little is left to the imagination.

In fact, some of the perversions in hardcore porn give you perverse ideas that you probably would not have had if you were not exposed to it.

After watching an hour and a half of nonstop sexual intercourse from camera angles that made everything bigger than life, I came out of the theater feeling disappointed from the first time experience. Instead of getting more aroused, a movie with only sexual intercourse as its plot, quickly became boring. So for the moment, I didn't pursue that avenue of pornography any further. Towards my latter years of college, maturity revealed that the reason I was not attracting quality women with depth and personality into my life was because of constant focus on the nude models in the porn magazines. Therefore, I was attracting only sex-crazed females who had no desire to be in a relationship other than sexual one.

And what did I care about having a relationship? Not much at the time. However, here is where I began to notice the dangerous side effects of pornography, in regards to women and relationships. Little did I know I was only steps away from a world of corruption I couldn't imagine.

Chapter Three
A World Full of Corruption

Out of college and on my own, I suddenly discovered that there were all kinds of corruption in the world that could feed my addiction. Now at the legal age of 21, life was filled with the forbidden fruit all around, which I felt I could now partake if I chose. I could confidently walk into the porn shops without being carded, I could go into nude bars, peep shows, even prostitutes look appealing. The choices were endless.

After a brief year of rest, a year after college, I picked up and moved to Texas to attend grad school. This was a new experience all by itself as most of the students in this school, men and women, were homosexuals.

During those days, I was very judgmental towards homosexuals, calling them a "virus which needed to be destroyed." Before then, I had only seen homosexuals in the music department during my undergraduate years but never came in personal contact with them.

In grad school, I had to interact and cohabitate with a homosexual roommate for an entire year. There were so few of us who were straight that we were considered the minority, which often lead to feelings of isolation and depression.

In a new city, where I knew no one, I would get in the car and drive around for hours looking for some kind of emotional lift. I frequently passed a few nude bars, which began to look more and more appealing as feelings of loneliness increased.

Finally, I stopped, took a deep breath and entered. Here in the nude bar, the waitresses were topless and the women dancing on the stage were topless with a g-string barely covering female genitals.

This was a new experience as the women were no longer on the pages of the magazine or on the big screen but live and in living color right in front of me. Their acts were erotic and seductive as they flirtatiously danced in your face or lap seeking to get a tip for their time. Though many of the women had exquisite bodies, their faces were hard from life in the fast lane. One young lady caught my attention because she was quite attractive with a body to match.

To me, she was a live version of the nude cuties in my favorite porn magazines. Because of that, I found myself frequenting this place almost every night of the week, not paying attention to how much money I was spending on the price of admission, drinks and tip for the dancer.

After a few weeks, I was beginning to make an emotional connection with this dancer because she was giving me more attention during her dances. It never dawned on me that she was doing this because I had become her favorite customer.

Nonetheless, I was feeling more and more attached emotionally. Finally, I got the nerve to ask her if she wanted to get together after she got off work. She reluctantly said "yes."

While waiting in the car for her to come out of the club, I felt really nervous as I had never done anything like this before. She finally came out and got in the car. We drove around for a while talking because I was having this intense inner battle about whether I should try to take her to my apartment or not. She was a college student making extra money. This girl was beautiful and soft, unlike the older dancers in the club hardened by time.

She now became nervous from all my questions and grew suspicious that I was an undercover cop trying to get information on her. She became so convinced of this that she asked that we call it a night and I just take her home.

Considering the inner battle I was having, I calmly agreed and took her home. I never returned to the bar after that because somehow, even back then, before being saved, I felt I was getting too close to the devil and backed off. I concluded that my magazines were much safer and less complicated and decided that they would be the vice I used to satisfy my continuous addiction.

Finally I began to date but my magazines were always close by. The physical perfection of the ladies in the porn magazines became a replacement of whatever physical qualities were missing in the ladies I was dating. This was extremely unfair to the young ladies I was dating as they were being compared to my fantasy relationship with the ladies in the magazines. I saw nothing wrong with that because, with the two, my needs were met. Of course, what was really happening here was that I was spiritually cheating on the women I dated because my other relationship was the constant fantasy I was having with the women in my porn magazines.

I finally met a nice young lady and got married, but never let told her about my addiction. At that time, I really didn't consider this an addiction.

I justified it by calling it a good way to help me stay true to my marriage; masturbating whenever I had an urge to cheat.

One day, my wife came home and found several pictorials lying on the dresser that I had forgotten to put away. She understood that men buy porn magazines but she was particularly disturbed that these magazines had no articles, only pictures.

I was so shocked I left the magazines out and my addiction was about to be revealed, to this day, I don't remember what lame excuse I gave her trying to explain why I was buying pictorials instead of the regular magazines.

It was at this time that my addiction was truly getting out of hand. I would have my encounters with the porn magazines all times of day, whenever I felt it was safe. It could be late at night when I was the only one awake, in the day when I was the only one at home, in the bathroom under the disguise that I was taking a long shower, and any other time I found convenient.

Other times, I found myself "going to the magazines" to relieve stress and anxiety. It really was no different from a person having a drink or smoking a joint to relieve stress. In my case, I was addicted to the natural chemical released by the brain's pleasure center during intercourse or self-gratification.

After seven years, I divorced my first wife for other reasons than the addiction, but my addiction was still intact. My relationship with porn magazines had now transferred to a means of stress reduction. Watching a talk show years later, I now realize I had become a sex addict. At the time, I thought sex addicts were those who were out of control addicted to having sex. However, if you stop and think about it, the same pleasure center in the brain is tapped when you masturbate as when you are having sexual intercourse. Sexual gratification is accomplished either way. The same chemical, from the pleasure center in the brain, is released in either case.

Therefore what the sex addict is addicted to, whether it is intercourse or masturbation, is the pleasure of sexual stimulation and the natural chemical, endorphins, released by the brain. As far as my actions were concerned, I might has well have been addicted to marijuana, cocaine, crack or any other drug.

If I had a big audition, I had to get my fix. If I had a big meeting, I had to get my fix. If I was feeling down and depressed, I had to get my fix. If I was bored, I had to get my fix. It got to a point where, self-gratification was the drug of my choice.

Now the really strange thing I discovered was that if a porn magazine was not handy, I could not successfully satisfy myself. It was my fantasy relationship with the nude models in the magazines that aroused me to the point I needed to achieve my goal. Thus my consistent use of the phrase "my relationship with porn magazines or nude dancers. It all began in my mind.

My mind had removed the urgent need to have a real woman in my life because that was too complicated. Women are just too moody, I concluded. My nude models in the magazines were there waiting for me and my fantasy, 24/7 if I so desired. Everything was sex related. If I did see an attractive woman, getting to know her beyond the desire to have sex with her never even crossed my mind. I didn't have time for all that and as a result decided my magazines were enough for now.

Shortly after my divorce I met a young lady who I was attracted to sexually and who had the same addiction to sex that I had. She was also like me in that she had no desire to get together for any other reason than to have sex. Wow, now I felt I was in paradise cause "ain't nothing like the real thing." It was almost like one of my fantasies had materialized out of one of the magazines and appeared right in front of me. The fact that she was an addict like me made my addiction even worse. We were feeding each other's addiction.

The void grew larger and larger until I began to pull away from the young lady and eventually broke it off so that I could evaluate this new desire to be emotionally close to someone. When you're trying to evaluate your emotions truthfully, it is impossible if sex is involved because your flesh is stronger and will cause you to evaluate your true emotions based on your sex life and not how you really feel. Of course, the young lady was upset with our break up but she understood.

Ironically, the Lord used this relationship to plant a major seed in my spirit. This young lady was very active in her church and I had been attending a religious science church for several years.

One night, after one of our climactic moments, out of the blue, she said, 'You really do need to get out of that cult and get back to Christianity." Well, I was really caught off guard and became very defensive. However, when I attempted to counter her debate, I suddenly realized that I had no idea of what religious science believed. I just thought it was a new age version of Christianity.

So, I postponed our debate until the following weekend so that I could get the religious science handbook and be ready to defend it the following weekend.

NOTES:

CHAPTER FOUR
A New Direction

During the following week, I went to the religious science bookstore and purchase their textbook so that I could come back well equipped for my debate.

Well, during our debate the previous weekend, A.L. had attacked religious science saying it was a cult because it was not Christianity, followers of Christ. Boy, was I ready to show her wrong and put an end to this line of discussion.

When I got the textbook, I went directly to the glossary and looked up "Christ". When I read their definition my mouth dropped to the floor. It was defined as "a change in spiritual awareness", i.e. Jesus didn't physically die but had a change of spiritual awareness, becoming Christ-like. That suddenly explained why we never had communion at the church I was attending. Another definition, "Hell is not a place but a state of mind." Wow, was I in the wrong place!

The following weekend, I admitted to my lady-friend that she was right and that I was going to join a traditional church as soon as possible. On that note, we never got together again physically, but on spiritual matters only. I suddenly felt spiritually overwhelmed and prayed, "Jesus, please don't return until I am back in the right place."

I began to visit church after church, trying to find one that I found spiritually satisfying. Slowly, my list of churches got shorter and shorter until I was down to two choices. Then I asked the Lord to guide me to the one I should join.

I ended up joining West Angeles Church of God in Christ, which gave me the strongest sense of spiritual peace of all my church visitations.

Though my most recent revelation ended the realm of "sex for the sake of sex", my old addiction with the magazines returned strong as ever, as if to say, "See, I told you dealing with women in person can get too complicated."

However, at the same time I was now truly trying to find a special woman with whom I could share strong feelings for the first time since my first love.

Several months went by and I found myself falling in love with another young lady, with whom I had much in common emotionally as well as physically. Again, I thought I had found the best of both worlds; physically compatible and in love. Man, this is the one. With all the emotions flowing and as a result, heighten physical intimacy, my pornography addiction continued but decreased somewhat. I was being satisfied in my relationship, physically and emotionally; something the magazines could not give me.

Excited about my newfound spiritual revelation. I decided that the only thing that could take this relationship to even another level was to worship together. Suddenly I realized that the one area where we were not compatible was spiritually.

I believed in going to church regularly. My girlfriend felt that regular church worship wasn't necessary as long as you believed and lived right. Though this bothered me a little, I justified it as being "not a problem" because my emotional and sex life was so good.

One day, I went to an interview with an elder at my church to be considered as a Sunday school worker. During the interview, I used the words "what I want" so much that the elder pointed it out to me and told me the importance of everything being about "what God wants."

Then he asked me about my girlfriend. I desperately tried to defend her beliefs about worship as one being in transition. The elder didn't buy it and stated that "it sounds like you two are unequally yoked."

Well, now I really got defensive. How dare him tell me that this is the wrong woman for me? He doesn't know what he's talking about. Our relationship is emotionally and spiritually sound. And that's that. What the elder had done was plant a seed into my spirit and made me realize that after being together for three years, I had no idea how I felt about spiritual issues.

Later that week, I decided to discuss a few Word-related issues with my girlfriend, just to prove the elder wrong. So I asked her how she felt about the Bible being the word of God. She replied that she didn't feel the Bible is the Word of God but more of a history book about the Word of God. The true Christian belief, of course, is that the Bible IS the Word of God.

For the first time since the revelation about being at the wrong church, I again felt, "Oh my God, I am in the wrong place." However, this time around, it was a little harder. In my stubbornness, I had decided that nothing could make this relationship any better. I had found a person with whom I was emotionally and physically compatible. What are the chances of finding someone who has those two qualities along with spiritual compatibility? Slim to none in my eyes! I wasn't willing to take that chance.

Unfortunately, it wasn't that simple. The meeting with the elder had set some things in motion spiritually that I wasn't even aware of. On a number of occasions, when I attempted to make sexual advances towards my lady-friend, she would say, "You sure you want to do this? I don't want to be the one to spoil your relationship with God!"

"Now why did she have to go and say that?" I would think to myself. Her statements would trigger an inner dialogue within me as to whether or not I should really be making those advances. The inner conflict would be so intense that it would completely smother my desire to have sex. This was my first realization that what's on your mind can really effect your sex life.

However, at that time, I was beginning to look at being saved as causing me more problems than good. Of course, that was mainly because I was being stubborn and rebellious in trying to be in control of the entire situation. Well, over the next several months, she and I had discussions on various spiritual issues. And each time, our conversation highlighted how different we were spiritually.

This became a major concern for me because at the time, my son was only seven years old. And in my mind, I was to hoping to marry this woman. If that happened, my son would be exposed to diverse spiritual viewpoints. I did not want that for him at such an early age. I wanted him to grow up being exposed to a single solid spiritual foundation.

From that point on over the next two or three months, my relationship with my girlfriend began to rapidly fall apart. The more it dissolved, the more I tried to be in control and the more it didn't work.

Finally, we broke up and I went into a deep depression for about six months. Being a poet, a lot of my therapy during this time was putting these feelings into poetry. It helped a little (see www.Poetry.com). But still, the depression lingered on. My old friend the "pornography addiction" returned full force in an attempt to forget or avoid the pain I was feeling inside. The depression was so bad I moved up to pornographic videos. That was even closer to the real thing because, like I said earlier, now the seductive, naked women were live and in living color.

My addiction was once again out of control. Whenever I felt depressed, which was most of the time, out came the magazine or the videos and I was off to have another self-gratifying experience. It got to a point where I would be totally exhausted from repeated sessions of self-gratification and would lie motionless in bed.

The cycles repeated so quickly that I was no different than a pothead who had smoked himself into a dazed stare.

There were times when I actually thought I heard the video tape in my drawer literally calling me, saying, "Hey, Fitz, it's that time again. You know you want to do it again. Come on! I'm waiting!" And like a mindless robot I would go to the draw, put on the tape and the cycle was on again.

I was totally out of control and knew it, but hadn't the slightest idea how to get control because of the depressed state I was in.

Even after all of that, the void inside was still winning no matter what I did. Finding peace of mind through the Word never crossed my mind.

The turning point for me was on one lonely, depressed night, I entertained the thought of killing myself. What else was left to live for in life? The love of my life was gone and surely I would never love again to fill this heart-wrenching void.

So I drove out to my favorite part of the beach, by the airport runway where you could see a beautiful view of the sunset and the ocean and, at the same time, watch the jets taking off. Normally, this was a comfort to me. But on this night it was now the perfect location to allow me peace and quiet so that I could decide which way I wanted to leave this world.

I had decided that speeding down a steep incline across two lanes of traffic and then crashing on the beach would be the way to go.

As I started the car, my heart began to race faster and faster, as my spirit was shouting, "DON'T DO IT!" "SHUT UP!" I responded. I was determined to carry out my fatal mission. "Why not do it? I have no one in my life to live for!" The pain from the heartbreak seemed unbearable. Finally, I decided to do it.

Then suddenly, the ocean seemed to disappear and a barrage of images of my son appeared before me. All of the good times we had shared and then images of him at my funeral and how devastated he would be if I did take my life. I turned off the car and broke down in tears. I don't know how long any of this took or how long I cried. But when it was over, I, at least, saw that there was a definite reason for me to stay in this world; my son.

Over the next five months, I lived in a "limbo" state of mind. I enjoyed my son's company, part-time, but my love life was non-existent. I kept hoping that somehow my relationship with A.D. could be reconciled but each time I tried it was clear that door was closed for sure.

During this time was I attempting to produce my first feature film. In the process, I was introduced by phone to Jahna, who was referred and described to me as an dynamic PR person to have on staff for my film. Whenever we talked, we would talk about my movie and then veer off and talk for another hour or two about all kinds of things in life. It was great therapy for me just to have someone to talk to with no intentions of developing a relationship.

Something was happening to me inside. During these same months of depression in limbo, the pornography addiction attempted to resurface as before. However, this time around, every time I opened the magazines to arouse myself, all kinds of scriptures filled my head to the point where my arousal completely left me. Those feelings were replaced by these two scriptures.

"Or do you not know that your body is the temple of the Holy Sprit who is in you, whom you have from God, and you are not of your own?"   *(1 Cor.6:19)*

"For if we sin willfully after we have received the knowledge of the truth, there no longer remains a sacrifice for sins, but a certain fearful expectation of judgment, and fiery indignation which will devour the adversaries."   *(Heb. 10:26-27)*

This began to happen more and more. It got to the point that each time I tried to look at a porn magazine or tried to watch an X-rated video, I felt like I was telling the Holy Spirit, "Excuse me, but could you step outside for a moment while I do this."

The embarrassment of this conversation in the spirit began to intimidate me to the point where my addiction to porn began a steady decline over the following months. Soon, I realized that whenever the strong urge to look at pornography for self-gratification would arise, reading or reciting scriptures was the perfect response that would finally give me power over the addiction. Because I was so depressed, this was a major challenge. Remember, my addiction like any other addiction, was fed by the desire to make myself feel better in a world of depression, no matter how temporary.

This period of depression, inner turmoil and spiritual stubbornness lasted for about six months. The thing that really gets me, as I look back, is that all this anguish was self-induced by my resisting God's plan to take me to the next level.

Within the next level was my next wife, a life of peace of mind, God's purpose for my life and much more.

However, I had delayed all that by being stubborn and angry for six months, insisting this was where I was suppose to be and that my ex-girlfriend had to be my next wife. If not her, who?

At the root of this behavior was the fact that I was not getting my way and was not in control of anything. The more I fought for control, the worse things got. So for me, the six months of depression and anguish was my version of Jonah in the belly of the whale for his disobedience.

Finally, at the New Year's Eve service at my church, I prayed, "Lord, I'm exhausted! Please lift this burden off my shoulders and give me peace of mind. What is it that I'm not doing? Where is it that you're trying to take me? Please help me!"

I'll never forget the service that night at church for there has never been one like it since. The service was the traditional service ending with a prayer for the New Year followed by praise and shouting. Following the benediction, the Minister of Music came to the mike and said, "I know many of you are ready to go out and do your own personal celebration but for those of you who don't have anywhere to go, we're going to stay here and do some more celebrating as well."

Well, of course, with nowhere to go and the way I was feeling, I chose to stay. And that decision ended up being the turning point in my life.

The church was rocking that night. There were four of us in the horn section and we played until our lips were about to fall off and we were about to collapse from exhaustion. But the Holy Spirit gave us the strength to keep on going.

A medley of singers praised and shouted for the next 3 hours and 45 minutes as yokes were being removed all over the sanctuary, mine included.

The service ended at 4 a.m. I was so exhausted that, to this day, I don't remember the drive home. What I do remember is that when I woke up the next day, I felt a hundred pounds lighter. Nothing had changed physically but spiritually I had been delivered from something. The depression was gone, anxiety was gone, the anger and hurt towards the relationship break up was gone and I felt I was literally experiencing the saying, "It's a brand new day" or, better yet, was it as the scriptures say, "Old things have passed away, behold all things become new." I didn't know where God was taking me but, praise God, I had finally let go of the past that was slowly killing me emotionally.

NOTES:

CHAPTER FIVE
(Uncharted Territory)

A few weeks later, on my way to the King Day Parade, an associate and I parked conveniently at my ex-girlfriend's house, only a few blocks away from the parade route. This was when I really realized that something had happened to me in that New Year's Eve service. When I saw her I felt no emotional attachment whatsoever. It was as if she had never been more than just a good friend. She even noticed my peaceful state of mind.

At the parade, I was to meet Jahna in person for the first time. Until now, we had only talked by phone over a period of about six months. It took quite a while to find her because she told me she would be dressed in a black sweatshirt with a gold studio emblem on the front.

I found this quite comical because there must have been a thousand or more other black women at the parade wearing some kind of black top or sweatshirt.

"She's got to be kidding. I'll never find her!" A friend of mind helped my search as one by one we repeatedly touched the wrong lady on the shoulder.

Finally, as I was just about to give up, I saw another black woman sitting on the curve several yards ahead of me but I didn't bother because, by that time, I felt I was never going to find who I was looking for.

The friend of mine who was helping me search, touched the woman on the shoulder and asked the same question we'd asked the other few hundred women. Only this time the response was, "Yes, that's me!" I was floored. The one woman I didn't question was the very one I was looking for. Moments later, as we chatted, we took a photo together and exchanged information, I remember thinking, "What a beautiful lady!" But I was in no emotional state to take that thought any further at that time.

Over the next few weeks, Jahna and I continued to talk on the phone and in person. Finally, I got the nerve to think, "Maybe she'll be interested in dating."

Boom, then came the old ways trying to sneak in again. "Hey, I wonder what's she's like in bed?"

"But I say to you that whoever looks at a woman to lust

for her has already committed adultery with her in his heart."

(Matt.5:28)

"No!" I shouted to myself. "I just got out of a relationship that was based on physical and emotional attraction without spiritual involvement. I want this one to be different."

So our first date was a night service at West Angeles. At first I thought, "Man, she's going to think I'm crazy asking her to go to church with me as a date."

But when I invited her, she happily said yes and added, "I've been wanting to go to a night service but could never get anyone to go with me."

So we instantly hit it off. I was now going where no Fitz had gone before, approaching a relationship from the spiritual point of view.

I felt so peaceful whenever I was with Jahna. Being with her felt so right and that really scared me. By April of that year, after only four months of dating I felt in my spirit, "This is the one I am to marry."

The ego responded, "That's impossible! You can't love this woman that soon. It's only been a few months since your last devastating breakup. You've got to mourn at least two years. Plus you still don't even know what this Jahna is like in bed."

"Hmmm! Maybe you're right!" I responded. "It is a little soon to be this much in love with someone. I must be on the rebound trying to get over the last relationship."

Well for the next six months, this conversation went back and forth about how serious I was about Jahna. Finally the Holy Spirit said, "What are you waiting for? You pray for the right woman, I lead her to you and now you're himmin' and hawin' about when to pop the question."

"You know what? You're right!" I said. So, on December 20, following the evening Christmas service, I proposed to her in the pew, right after the benediction. Jahna was in shock, but I figured if church was where we started dating, what better place for the proposal. We set the date for May 22, 1993 which didn't give us much time because most deadlines for reserving this or that was only a month or two away. On top of that, if we wanted our Bishop to marry us, we had to take a mandatory eight-week pre-marital counseling class.

By now you may have noticed that I haven't mentioned anything about my addiction for quite some time. It was still in the back of my mind, but finally I had control of it. That leads to my next point.

During all these months, the Word was at the head of both of our lives. There were a few times when the addiction sneaked in there and got me during a few weak moments which truly enhanced scripture that we must "Pray without ceasing." In fact several scriptures came to mind each time the spirit of lust tried to enter my mind.

"...Rejoice always, pray without ceasingin everything give thanks, for this is the will of God in Christ Jesus for you."   *(1 Thess.5:16-18)*

"Be sober, be vigilant; because your adversary the devil walks about like a roaring lion, seeking whom he may devour."   *(1 Peter 5:8)*

"Therefore, submit to God. Resist the devil and he
will flee from you. Draw near to God and He will
draw near to you..."

(James 4:7-8)

Whatever your vice, the enemy is monitoring your thoughts and fleshly desires, 24/7, just waiting for you to have a weak moment; and then, BOOM, you slip. Whenever that happens, repent and get back in sync. If you are sincere about living by the Word and your repentance is from the heart, the Lord knows and Holy Spirit will continue to strengthen you more and more each time until those "slip-ups" are no more unless YOU allow them.

"If we say that we have no sin, we deceive ourselves
and the truth is not in us. If we confess our sins, He
is faithful and just to forgive us our sins and to cleanse
us from all unrighteousness."   *(1 John 1:8)*

"Walk in the Spirit, and you shall not fulfill the lust
of the flesh. For the flesh lusts against the Spirit and
the Spirit against the flesh; and these are contrary
to one another, so that you do not do the things that
you wish."   *(Gal.5:17)*

"For all that is in the world – the lust of the flesh, the
lust of thee yes, and the pride of life – is not of the Father
but is of the world. And the world is passing away, and
the lust of it; but he who does the will of God abides forever."
(1 John 2:16-17)

Now once you are in total control of the flesh and you then choose to sin, that's a different story.

"For if we sin willfully after we have received the knowledge of the truth, there no longer remains a sacrifice for sins, but a certain fearful expectation of judgment, and fiery indignation which will devour the adversaries."   (Heb. 10:26-27)

NOTES:

CHAPTER SIX

So Where Do You Go From Here?

So after all that has been said, what do you do now? Now we come to the most important step and the purpose for writing this book and sharing all this with you.

You must now evaluate yourself honestly and identify any and all lusts that are active in your life. You may slip into a state of denial at first and that is quite natural. Remember, it was my struggle with denial that blocked God's instructions for almost four years before I could write this book, but in the end the truth forced its way out like a volcanic eruption.

The longer you try to hide the truth within, the bigger the inner struggle. Over time that struggle must be resolved in order to achieve peace of mind. On separate sheets of paper, write down the following:

(1)   List everything you lust for, from strongest to the weakest. Be honest. The name of each lust is at the top

(2)   Under each lust listed, write down how often this lust is on your mind. Also, note the time of day or environment when this lust strikes. Is it consistent, irregular or is it triggered by something?

(3)   When this lust strikes, how strong is its hold on you? Does it feel uncontrollable, at its peak?

(4)   Does this lust have a negative effect on your relationship or viewpoint towards a loved one, especially your spouse or significant other?

(5)   Are you aware of when this lust is about to strike or does it blindside you? If it blindsides you, what kept you from seeing it coming?

(6)   As this lust begins to come over you, do you try to resist it or just give in and let it take control?

(7)   Is there any activity in your life that feeds this lust?

(8)   Is the activity that feeds this lust any kind of addiction?

(9)   Up to this point, have you sincerely attempted to be delivered from this lust?

(10)   How long have you been dealing with this lust? How old were you when this lust came into your life?

(11)   Are you sincerely ready, from this point on, to take control of that lust and put it under your feet?

Now that you have answered these questions regarding the lust(s) you have identified on those sheets of paper, the first major step has been taken. Hopefully, after these questions, you not only know what lusts are active in your life but also which one has the most control over you. Now you're ready to do battle.

CHAPTER SEVEN

The good news is that you can defeat the strongest lust as easily as you can defeat the weakest. We're now expanding beyond pornography and including all forms of lust. What game plan to you use to take control of these lusts?

(1)   You must sincerely make the commitment that you wish to take control of lust and get it out of your life.

(2)   Know that the Word of God has power over any lust that can come your way.

(3)   You must replace any activity in your life that is feeding the lust.

(4)   Every lust is drawn in by a receptive mindset which openly allows the body to enjoy it.

(5)   You must have an artillery of scriptures at the tip of your tongue the very second that a lustful thought comes into your mind. Over time this act will not allow your mind to entertain a lustful thought.

(6)   Next, repeat the scriptures over and over again, as many times as it take to get the thought out of your mind. Each time the lust returns If the lust has manifested in the body it will have less and less effect on the body.

(7)   Once you are being delivered from lust, you must never let your guard down and keep the Word in your life, daily. Remember, the devil is working 24/7 and waiting for you to slip up and forget so that he can insert a lustful thought. If that happens, get busy repeating your scriptures and chase that lustful thought out.

(8)   Also, once you are delivered, do not flirt with the lust by engaging in activities that can easily feed the lust. For ex; If you're trying to stop eating donuts, you don't celebrate your new discipline by taking your lunch break in a donut shop. You're setting yourself up for failure if you do that.

(9)   Immerse yourself with the Word daily, through audio and video-taped sermons, books, radio and television ministries and gospel music as well as spending quality time praying or conversing with God daily.

(10)   You MUST commit to the discipline of following ALL of the steps mentioned above if you truly want to take control of your life and keep lustful thoughts at bay.

Child of God, as God is my witness, this works, but only if you truly want to be delivered. As with anything else, if you go into it half-heartedly, then very little will be accomplished. This is a serious matter. "Lusts of the flesh" is one of the devil's most powerful weapons used to try to keep us separated from God. If he can keep us separated from God then we'll never hear God's voice and respond obediently, which is where all His blessings lie. If he can keep us separated from God, we'll never know God as loving and merciful because we'll be busy blaming God for our failures.

Make the commitment to yourself and God right now that you will do what it takes to be delivered from the lust that haunts you. Let us pray!

Father, in the name of Jesus, I come before you willingly, and ask for deliverance from the lust that has been haunting me. As your word says, "I can do all things through Christ who strengthen me."

Lord, I lift up to all of my lusts, which I have been entertaining for much too long. I give them all to you knowing, at the same time, that they shall no longer have control over me, in the name of Jesus.

In the name of Jesus, I claim my victory over every lust that comes my way and put them all under my feet this day. They have no control over me from this day forward, in the name of Jesus. I cast _every lustful thought out of my head immediately, in the name of Jesus. And I commit to living my life for you, realizing that my body is a temple which will be respected as much as I respect you, in the name of Jesus, I pray, amen!_

NOTES:

CHAPTER EIGHT
Scriptures for your Battle with Lust

The following are just a few of many scriptures that can be helpful in leading you to victory over lust of the flesh. Feel free to add any of your favorite scriptures to the ones below. But once your tongue is loaded and ready to speak the Word at a moments notice, then you'll not only have an upper hand on lust, but you will also have victory in many other areas of your life as well.

"I can do all things through Christ who strengthens me."
(Phil.4:13)

"My God shall supply all my need according to His riches in glory by Christ Jesus." *(Phil. 4:19)*

"And now to you, O Lord, who is able to do exceedingly and abundantly above all we can ask or think according to the power that works in me."

(Eph. 3:20)

"But I say to you that whoever looks at a woman to lust for her has already committed adultery with her in his heart"
(Matt. 6:28)

"Beloved, I beg you as sojourners and pilgrims, abstain from fleshly lusts which war against the soul."

(1 Peter 2:9)

"Marriage is honorable among all, and the bed undefiled; but fornicators and adulterers God will judge."   *(Heb. 13:4)*

"Blessed is the man who endures temptation; for when he has been approved, he will receive the crown of life which the Lord has promised to those who love Him."   *(James 1:12)*

"For this is the will of God, your sanctification that you should abstain from sexual immorality; that each of you should know how to possess his own vessel in sanctification and honor, not in passion of lust, like the Gentiles who do not know God."   *(1 Thess. 4:5)*

"Or do you not know that your body is the temple of the Holy Sprit who is in you, whom you have from God, and you are not of your own?"   *(1 Cor.6:19)*

"For if we sin willfully after we have received the knowledge of the truth, there no longer remains a sacrifice for sins, but a certain fearful expectation of judgment, and fiery indignation which will devour the adversaries."   *(Heb. 10:26-27)*

"...Rejoice always, pray without ceasing in everything give thanks, for this is the will of God in Christ Jesus for you."   *(1Thess.5:16-18)*

"Be sober, be vigilant; because your adversary the devil walks about like a roaring lion, seeking whom he may devour." *(1 Peter 5:8)*

"Therefore, submit to God. Resist the devil and he will flee from you Draw near to God and He will draw near to you..." *(James 4:7-8)*

"If we say that we have no sin, we deceive ourselves and the truth is not in us. If we confess our sins, He is faithful and just to forgive us our sins and to cleanse us from all unrighteousness." (1 John 1:8)

"Walk in the Spirit, and you shall not fulfill the lust of the flesh. For the flesh lusts against the Spirit and the Spirit against the flesh; and these are contrary to one another, so that you do not do the things that you wish." (Gal.5:17)

"For all that is in the world – the lust of the flesh, the lust of the eyes, and the pride of life – is not of the Father but is of the world. And the world is passing away, and the lust of it; but he who does the will of God abides forever." (1 John 2:16-17)

"But fornication and all uncleanness or covetousness, let it not even be named among you, as is fitting for saints, neither filthiness, nor foolish talking, nor coarse jesting, which are not fitting, but rather giving thanks. For this you know, that no fornication unclean person, nor covetous man, who is an idolater, has any inheritance in the Kingdom of Christ and God." (Eph.5:3-5)

NOTES:

CHAPTER NINE
Statistics on the Pornography Industry

I've shared with you the effects pornography had on my life. I think it is only fair to share with you some of the disturbing statistics regarding the pornography industry so that you may understand the magnitude of the devastation caused by this powerful vice.

THE IMMENSITY OF THE BUSINESS OF PORNOGRAPHY

Last year's online pornography market in the United States is conservatively estimated at $175 million in revenue, some reported as high as 200 million to 1 billion per year.

--- David Card, Researcher at N.Y.-based Jupiter Communications;--- N2H2 press release, 8 / 01 ---

The pornography industry took in another $8 billion in 1999; more than all revenues generated by rock-&-roll and country music, more than America spent on Broadway productions, theater, ballet, jazz and classical music combined.

----"Porn.com 'US News & World Report" (3 / 00) ---

Internet Population:

1- 12	11.7 mil (14.5%)
13 – 17	11.1 mil (13.7%)
18 – 34	23 mil. (28.5%)
35 – 54	25 mil (31.2%)
55 +	23 mil (21.1%)

--The Definition Guide to Who's Who Online in the US and What They Do" The eMarketer Stat   Store (taken from eMarketer) 9/99

Sex is the number 1 searched for topic on the Internet.

---- Dr. Robert Weiss, Sexual Recovery Institute, Washington Times, 1/26/2000)   ----

60% of all websites are sexual in nature.

--- (MSNBC / Stanfordl/Dusquesne Study, Washington Times) –

There was a 345% increase in child pornography.

(2/2000 – 7/2000)   --N2H2 press release, 8/01) -

Cyber- sex is the crack cocaine of sexual addiction. It reinforces and normalizes sexual disorders.

--- (Dr. Robert Weiss, "Sexual Recovery Inst.) Washington Times --- (1/2/2000)

Cyber-sex is a public health hazard exploding because very few are recognizing it as such or taking it seriously.   57 million American have Internet access.

----- (MSNBC / Stanford/Dusquesne Study, 2000)-

200,000 internet users are hooked on porn sites, x-rated chats, or other sexual materials online.   – MSNBC- --

63% of men attending "Men, Romance & Integrity" Seminars admit to struggling with porn in the last year.

--- (Christian Today, Leadership Survey, Dec.2001)

INTERNET EXPOSURE FACTS

     A new study released by the "Family Research Council Dangerous Access, 2000 edition: Upcoming Internet pornography in

America's Libraries," says that the American Library Association is ignoring a "sea of evidence" that Internet porn and related sex crimes are a serious problem in America's libraries.

With only 29% of libraries responding, researchers found 3000 incidents of patrons, many of them children, accessing pornography in America's public libraries.

(http://orlandosentinel.com/news/031900-parker.htm) --3/19/00 --

Sexual content on prime-time TV more than tripled in the past 10 years. --- "More TV Sex" (USA today) – 3/30/00 ---

The National Council in Sexual Addiction Compulsivity estimated 6-8% of Americans are sex addicts (which =16-21 million people). --- Taken from Amparano,J. "Sex Addicts Get Help" p.A1 (1999)

26 popular children's characters, such as Pokemon, My Little Pony, and ACTION MAN, revealed thousands of links to porn sites. 30% of those links were "Hard Core." --- (Envisional 2000) -

51% of pastors say cyber-porn is a possible temptation while 37% say it is a current struggle. 4 in 10 pastors have visited a porn site. - Christian Today, Leadership Survey, Dec.2001–

Pornographers disguise their sites (i.e. Stealth Sites), with common brand names, including Disney, Barbie, ESPN, etc to entrap children. ---(Cyveilance Study, March 1999) ---

31% of kids 10-17 from homes with computers (24% of all kids, 10-17) say they have seen a pornographic site. -- "Survey Shows Widespread Enthusiasm for High Technology" NPR online. http://www.npr.org/programs/special/poll/techonology (taken from a new poll by Nation Public Radio, the Kaiser Family Foundation & Harvard's Kennedy School of Govt.) 1999

Nationwide survey of 1,031 adults conducted by Zogby International in 2000 found that 20% admitted visiting a sexually oriented site. 37% of males, 18-24, admitted they had visited sex sites; of those 18% were Christians and 18% were married men.)

-Zogby Focus Survey Reveals Shocking Internet Sex Stats."

-Legal Facts: Family Research Council.,Vol.2, No.20. (3/30/00)

The statistics go on and on. For more statistics, enter "pornography statistics" in the Search Box on your internet provider. However, from the statistics I have mentioned in this chapter, I think you can see how, through the expansion of technology via the internet, pornography's reach is threatening to reach out into our very homes and plant the seed of the spirit of lust into the very heart of family life.

May the Lord bless you and keep you as we claim victory, in advance, over all destructive spirits of lust of the flesh, named and unnamed, in the name of Jesus. Amen!

CHAPTER TEN
Self-evaluation & observation

This section of the book is to ask yourself questions that pertain to all the different ways pornography can sneak into your life. If you are not aware of what to watch out for, you can be blind-sided and end up entertaining the "lust of the flesh" unaware.

Most importantly, be honest with yourself. There is no healing power in denial. It is only when you examine your true feelings that you can find any area of weakness and correct it accordingly.

1. Do you enjoy looking at the bra section in department store catalogs?

    _____

    _____

2. Do you find yourself drawn to buying any or all, of the magazines which have a swimsuit issue?   Any particular magazine, and why? _____

    _____

3. Do you buy certain magazines especially because of the swimsuit centerfold included inside?

    _____

4. Do you find that the swimsuit issue models arouse you and that you cannot stop looking at the pictures?

    _____

    _____

5. Do the models in the swimsuit issues or the centerfold magazines cause you to fantasize about having sex with a woman like the model?

    _____

6.   Are you at a point where the swimsuit issues and centerfold magazines are boring and your body craves to see even more flesh?_____

If yes, do you give in to the craving and buy pornography magazines in order to enjoy your ever-growing fantasies?

_____

7.   Do any of the magazines previously mentioned, lingerie catalogs, swimsuit issues, centerfold magazines or pornography magazines, sexually arouse you enough to masturbate?

_____

_____

8.   Do you buy pornography pictorial magazines (pictures only) instead of ornography magazines with articles?

_____

_____

9.   Do you view women as sex objects?

_____

10.   Do you look at your wife or-girlfriend and wish they looked like the swimsuit or porn models?

_____

11.   Which sexually arouses your more, your wife

or girlfriend; or the swimsuit and porn models?

_____

_____

12.   Do you have trouble getting aroused by your wife or girlfriend without looking at swimsuits issues or porn magazines first?

_____

_____

13. Do you like to rent X-rated movies? _____

14. Do you need X-rated movies or magazines in order to arouse yourself enough to have sex?

   _____

   _____

15. Are you able to masturbate without a magazine or video? __

   _____

16. Do internet pornography site invitations cause you to have a battle with temptation? _____

17. Have you ever visited a pornography site? _____

18. Have you or do you belong to a porn site(s)? _____

19. Do you have a pornography screen-saver? _____

20. Is your addiction to pornography a secret? _____

21. Do you feel you are addicted to pornography?

   _____

22. Do you want to be delivered from the spirit of pornography?

   _____

23. Are catalogs, swimsuit issues and centerfold magazines lying around your house, where they can be easily seen by

   young kids? _____

24. Are you aware that scriptures and the "spirit of lust" occupy the body at the same time? _____

25. Have you answered these question truthfully_____

In conclusion, YOU ARE ADDICTED IF;

--- your body craves to look at pornographic pictures or movies as much or more than you crave to be with your wife or girlfriend.

---you compare your wife or girlfriend with the porn magazine or movie models.

---you expect your wife or girlfriend to behave like the porn magazine or movie models.

---if you cannot masturbate without porn or swimsuit issue.

-- you fantasize having sex with the porn or swimsuit issue models.

---you crave the porn and swimsuit magazines in order to

masturbate when you're stressed.

---you can't stop looking at the pictures in porn or swimsuit issue magazines.

---you can hear the porn magazines or videos calling out to you like a drug addict.

If you are not addicted, drop on your knees and thank the Lord. If you are addicted, I'm here to tell you that keeping the Word in your heart will keep the "spirit of lust" out of your life. However, just like the verse says, "pray without ceasing", so you must realize that the second you get lazy about keeping the Word on your tongue at all times, that's the second that the "spirit of lust" will attempt to return and once again get a hold of you.

Once delivered from this addiction, remember, you must see to it that you do not keep magazines, videos, and anything else around you, from the addicted times, that can invite the "spirit of lust" to return. That includes the kinds of friends you hang around, the kinds of activities you get involved in, as well as enticing environments that remind you of your former lustful life. When you're trying not to eat donuts, you don't sit outside the donut shop and enjoy the aroma. YOU GET AWAY FROM IT!!

Yes, it's going to take discipline, on your part, but there's nothing like the feeling of knowing that you are once again in control of your body's desires and not a slave to your body's desires.

At this point I would also like to note that my deliverance (without therapy) is not considered the norm and nothing less that a miracle. Even though the Lord reached down and pulled me out of the darkness, I often wonder how much sooner I would have been delivered if I had had the nerve to ask for help. Should you need one on one counseling, 12-step or even a buddy system to work through the addiction, do it. This is NOT something to fight on your own. You must treat this addiction as seriously as you would treat a drug addict trying to get off coke or any other drug.

YOU CAN DO IT! I am living proof. Your first step is admitting you have this addiction and then attack it head on.

May the Lord bless you and keep you!

NOTES & CONTACT INFO FOR COUNSELING OR SUPPORT GROUPS

ABOUT THE AUTHOR

This is the first published work by Fitzhugh G. Houston. An accomplished actor, screenwriter and musician. He received his B.A. from Hampton University and M.F.A. from Dallas Theater Center, which was formally affiliated with Trinity University. Houston and his wife, Jahna, have been active members of West Angeles Church of God in Christ for over a decade, where he played trumpet and flugelhorn with the worship service band. He is a gospel-jazz rap & flugelhorn artist, and has just completed production on three debut CDs, *"INTERLUDES I & II,"* and *"RAPPIN' AND PRAISIN' HIS NAME*. The two Houstons also perform together as a praise and worship duo *The Sounds of Faith*. Houston currently stars in the independent films *The Deposition, Get Thee Behind Me, Just Another Day* and the critically acclaimed short film *Cold Comfort*. Houston's television credits include a recurring role on *The Michael Richards Show,* co-starring roles on *JAG, That's So Raven, Malcolm in the Middle, Robbery Homicide Division, The District, The X-Files, Judging Amy, Family Law, Sister Sister, The Parent 'Hood, Sparks, ROC, 227, Married With Children.*

Some of Houston's theater credits include Proposals, (Best Supporting Actor Award 2001) Fences, Once on This Island, the Wiz in The Wiz; The Amen Corner; the original gospel musical, For This Reason, the national touring production of Woman of the Year starring Lauren Bacall.

Houston and his wife, Jahna have been married for eleven years and reside in southern California. She is the reigning Mrs. Volunteer America. He is the proud dad of Jonathan, a graduate of Tuskegee University, class of 2004. For more information and credits, log on to; http://www.fitzhouston.net

HSU

HOUSTON SPECTRUM PUBLICATIONS

<u>To Order Copies of this Book</u>

For mail order:
Send a money order for $9.95
plus $3.95 for shipping and handling to;

Fitzhugh G. Houston
Faith Hope Help Ministries
9301 Van Nuys Blvd. Ste. 245
Panorama City, CA. 91402

or
TO ORDER ONLINE
visit
www.menletstalk.org
please allow 2-4 weeks for delivery

OTHER PRODUCTS
BY
FITZ HOUSTON
From
Houston Spectrum Publishing

GUIDED TO THE LIGHT Book One
by Fitzhugh G. Houston

A Christian actor/musician's inspirational testimony of lessons and experiences, from his dark days of worldly living, to how he was guided to the light of God's Word, where he found joy and peace, while moving closer to God.   **Price $10.00**

DIVINE RHYMES
by Fitzhugh G. Houston

DIVINE RHYMES is a collection of 52 poems consisting of poetic prayers, conversations with God, spiritual streams of consciousness and testimonies seeking to pull the reader to a closer relationship with God by sharing the author's journey through life with the Word.   **Price $10.00**

DIVINE RHYMES II
By Fitzhugh G. Houston

Fifty inspirational poems, on a variety of subjects, continue to flow from the author of DIVINE RHYMES, touching on emotions of every kind as God reveals His viewpoint or participation in our lifes though poetry. "May these divinely inspired poems be a blessing to all who read them as much as they have been a blessing to me writing them." **From: $10.00**

LESSONS IN LIFE
by Fitzhugh G. Houston

LESSONS IN LIFE, poems about life, love and relationships, is a collection of poems which share the author's life experiences and touches a variety of emotions, capturing the very essence of those moments in time.   Price $10.00

For information about Fitz's CDs, click on;

www.christianproductsbyfitz.com